MARGARET SILF
ON
PRAYER

A LION BOOK

A Lion Book
an imprint of
Lion Hudson plc
Mayfield House, 256 Banbury Road,
Oxford OX2 7DH, England
www.lionhudson.com
ISBN 0 7459 5132 5

First edition 2004
10 9 8 7 6 5 4 3 2 1 0

A catalogue record for this book is available
from the British Library

Typeset in 11/13 Goudy Old Style
Printed and bound in Malta

Contents

'Prayer is a means by which I open myself to that which is not me.'

Alan Jones

Introduction

Prayer is a mystery.

Prayer is a process we don't understand,
leading us more deeply into a Mystery
we don't understand.

Just to think about prayer is to
open up so many questions...

What is prayer, and why do we do it,
or wish we could do it,
or feel we are missing out on something
when we don't do it?

How do we pray?
How do we begin to turn the deepest stirrings inside us
into the words
and the silences
of prayer?

Who do we think we are praying to?
And who do we want to be praying for?

Where is the place for prayer?
Is it just something for the church, or the 'holy place'?
Or can prayer be real on the pavements, at the work
    station, in the traffic jam?

Is prayer just for the good days, when our hearts want to
    sing out for joy?
Or dare we throw the book at God,
let God take the brunt of our anger,
the cold of our fears,
the dull thump of our daily frustrations?

Does prayer flow in all its power
    only when the sunset is golden,
    the longed-for child is born,
    or the world is going our way,

or also when the plane has been hijacked,
    the child is stillborn,
    the doors of redundancy have closed behind us?

In this little book we will explore some of these questions.

But any answers you discover will be your own,
because prayer is itself a journey of discovery,
an experience unique to each one of us,
a personal relationship
with the God beyond our understanding
and the God who dwells in the core of our being,
closer to us than our own heartbeat,
the God our minds can never fathom,
yet our hearts can *know*.

All that this book can give you is a few footprints,
a few hints from the experience of those who have made
   the journey of prayer before us,
and a little encouragement to risk...

... the adventure of prayer.

What is prayer?

The definitions of prayer that have been formulated
    through the ages
would easily fill a shelf, if not a library.

Prayer has a life of its own.
If we could define it today,
that definition would have moved and changed
    by tomorrow.
Prayer is a living relationship that can never be
    pinned down and analysed,
Prayer is a breath of the soul that has passed
    before we can seize hold of it,
Prayer is a reaching out of all that is deepest within us
towards all that lies infinitely beyond and around us.

Take a few moments to ponder what prayer means,
    right now, to *you*.

Some things can perhaps be said about prayer,
drawn from the well of human experience
    through the ages.

These are just a few ways of looking at prayer.

They are not the final word on anything,
but only a first tentative gathering
of what many people find prayer means for them.

Prayer is about belonging…

When we look out through a telescope into the far reaches
   of our universe,
we see a vast reality beyond ourselves,
and beyond the reaches of our minds
   or even our imagination,
yet we are part of that reality.
We belong to it.
We live and move and have our being within it.

When we gaze into a microscope, at just a single cell
   in our own body,
we also see an immensity of life and interrelatedness
   beyond our wildest dreams,
a world of its own, a minuscule microcosm of that
   vast outer reality.
It lives and moves and has its being in us.
It is a living part of who we are.

Whether we look outwards, or inwards, everything belongs.
Everything is in relationship with everything else.
This reality is what many people would call 'God'.
God who holds everything in being,
continually impelling all creation in the direction of Life.

Prayer is our response to this reality,
our expression of our deep desire to be in right relationship
   with its Source and Sustainer.
This in turn can lead us into right relationship with
   each other and with the world.

Prayer is about coming to stillness…

We have largely grown up, especially in the western world,
with the idea that to have value we must be busy,
or at least appear to be busy.
I work, therefore I am!

We tend to identify ourselves in terms of what we do
    for a living.
We feel a bit guilty if we spend too long just dreaming,
or reading a book,
or smelling the roses,
or gazing at the seashore.

It's not difficult to understand why our view of prayer
    has fallen into the same way of thinking.
We feel we need to be filling our prayer time
    with clever words,
as if a well-turned phrase has greater power to capture
    God's attention.

Or we measure the 'success' of our prayer by the time
    we have spent on it,
or the degree of discomfort we feel
at the end of an hour kneeling in a cold church.

Prayer is about listening…

But what if prayer were more about listening to God
   in the silence of our hearts,
than about bombarding God with our piety?

Imagine a glass of muddy water.
When you look into it, you can see nothing through
   the cloudiness.
But if you leave the glass alone for a while,
and allow the water to become perfectly still,
you will see how the mud settles
and the water becomes crystal clear.

Prayer time and prayer space can be like that water.
If we let ourselves come to rest,
to a state of physical and mental equilibrium,
the ocean within us will become calmer and clearer,
and we will be better able to pick up the still small voice
which is God's whisper in our heart.

Coming to stillness is a skill we can cultivate,
as we shall see later.

Prayer is about living reflectively…

When the ocean within us becomes still and clear,
we can begin to see things as they really are,
in ourselves, and in our world.

During a time of stillness,
while we are open and receptive to the voice of God within us,
we may discover new ways forward in the situations that
    concern us,
or a challenge to change our attitude in some relationship,
or to turn our compassion for a friend into practical action.

This alone won't move any mountains.
We need to chew over whatever opens up for us in prayer,
and reflect on what it means for us in practice,
and how it connects to our daily living.

Without this ongoing reflectiveness
our prayer becomes, literally, 'disembodied'.
The reflection, as we move on with our daily life,
is what weaves the wisdom of God into our moment-by-
    moment choices and decisions,
our reactions, responses and relationships.

Prayer, then, is not something we *do*,
but a way of living,
in growing awareness of the greater reality
in which we live and breathe.

Prayer is a gift, not an achievement...

Before we move on,
there is one more commonly held notion
that we may need to let go.

We were told from earliest childhood
that we would have to work to achieve our dreams.
Our so-called work ethic
is all about personal achievement.

No wonder, then, that we expect prayer to work
   the same way.
The harder we work at it, we think,
the better it will be.
If it doesn't seem to be 'working', it must be our fault.
We must be doing something wrong.

But suppose prayer were more like love than work?
Suppose it were something that is simply given,
and all we are asked to do is to be open to receive it,
and respond to the gifting?

There is nothing we can do to earn another person's love,
or to achieve it by hard work,
or pass an exam to obtain it,
or compel it in any way.

We can only receive it with a joyful heart,
and respond to it with a generous life.

And so it is with prayer.

Prayer is God's gift,
and never our own 'achievement'.

Everybody who ever tries to pray
is convinced that everyone else is doing it better!

It isn't true, of course,
because the love of God is the ocean in which we all swim.
All we can do is become more aware
of the reality of that ocean
and let this awareness inform the way we live.

Why would I pray?

There are as many reasons to pray as there are people
  on the planet.

Perhaps we were taught to pray as children.
Prayer was part of the bedtime ritual.
But we may well have lost the habit
and sometimes wish we could rediscover it.

Or we may be used to prayer in a formal religious setting.
It seems fine while we are in the 'holy place'.
But does it have any meaning in our daily lives, as they are
  actually lived?
Perhaps we are looking for some way of praying that will be
  meaningful right through the week
and not just on high days and holy days.

None of us can go back.
Prayer needs to grow with us,
if it is to be meaningful in our adult lives.
Later in this book we will explore some of the ways
in which that growth might happen.

Meanwhile, we might well ask:
what makes us want to pray at all?
Why does it feel important?
What is it really all about?

Because I am searching for right relationship

Human beings are relational creatures.
We long to belong.
For this reason we make friends
and look for love.
This is what binds us together in families
and in communities.

Yet our human relationships rarely live up to their promises.
Friends let us down, and love can disappoint us.
Families grow up and move away
and communities break apart.
But the longing to belong never goes away.

Such a longing is not just some vague yearning for what
    can never be.
It is the voice of our collective human heart,
telling us that right relationship is actually at the heart
    of the matter
and that we must keep striving for it, whatever life
    throws at us.

One reason why we pray is because we sense
that this right relationship is to be found
only in the mystery we call God.
We intuit that 'everything belongs'
and that all life is interrelated and interdependent.
In prayer we seek to come close to the heart
    of that wholeness,
and allow our own lives to be touched by it,
and even transformed by it.

Because I long for true communication

Relationship requires communication.
We talk with our friends,
we share the most important issues of our lives with them
and we are comfortable just to be silent with them.
We allow them to see us as we really are,
not trying to hide the bits we don't like.
And they accept us just as we really are,
loving us in spite of everything.

If God is real,
and if God is the all-embracing presence,
the ambience of accepting unconditional love
that we believe God is,
then to be in relationship with God also means
talking with God,
listening to God,
sharing the most important issues in our lives with God,
not hiding anything,
trusting that we are welcome just as we are.

So a powerful reason to pray
is to nourish this relationship.

The more we nourish it,
the more we discover that actually it is the relationship
    with God that is nourishing *us*.

Because I am searching for meaning

Another distinctive feature of the human heart and mind
is our desire to discover meaning.

Every moment we learn more and more of the hidden
    meanings woven into the created world that is our home.
We strive to penetrate the mysteries of mathematics
    and music,
and we sense that the discipline of order and meaning
is also a gateway to immense freedom and creativity.

To be alive in a universe that reveals its meanings to us,
through science and through art,
through the life and growth of all creatures
and through our own attempts to live our lives
according to values of harmony and cooperation,
is to ponder the source of these underlying meanings in
    the mystery of things.

Such pondering turns to prayer,
as we realize that the Meaning is something
so much bigger than our own small minds can fathom.

Our search for meaning is a reason to pray.

Because I am looking for guidance

Our universe is utterly beautiful
and utterly bewildering in its immensity.

Our lives, too, though pregnant with wonder,
are also fraught with ambiguity,
dilemmas
and every kind of impasse.

Every day we face choices and decisions,
and there is rarely a 'right' answer,
or an obvious way forward.

And so we long for direction,
for guidance through this labyrinth of life.
We search for the truths deep within us and beyond us
that will guide us in the wisest course.

Our constant search for guidance
is a reason why we pray.

Because my heart is overflowing

There are times when we feel, quite simply, far too small
to contain everything we are feeling.

Maybe a moment of awesome beauty overwhelms us,
or a piece of music brings tears to our eyes.

We hold a newborn child in our arms
and are lost for words.
We gaze, helplessly, as a loved one takes a final breath.

Or maybe we are speechless with rage,
impotent in the face of some gross injustice,
or some intolerable pain.

Prayer can catch us in its arms at times like these,
often in shared rituals or rites of passage,
but also in the unspoken, and unspeakable,
achings and yearnings of our hearts.

We pray when our hearts are overflowing.

Because I am at the limits

'Human extremity is God's opportunity.'
Often prayer is our response to the extreme situations
   in life.
People who never pray,
pray when the chips are down.

Is this cheating?
Those who pray faithfully every day may think so.
But once there was a thief, who was caught in the act,
and hanged, alongside Jesus, on a cross to die.
He may never have uttered a prayer in his life,
but he prayed that afternoon.
He cried out to the dying Jesus, hanging next to him:
'I deserved it,' he said, 'but you did nothing but good.'

Jesus heard this prayer.
'Trust me,' he whispered.
'We are travelling together to where this all makes sense.'

When the worst happens,
and it is worse even than anything we could
   have imagined,
then a sword pierces our togetherness,
and prayer spills out of us.

Perhaps no prayer is more authentic
than prayer at the extremes of human experience,
where our very worst comes face to face with our very best,
and something new is born of that union.

Because I feel compassion

Pain can be a friend in disguise.
It warns us that something is wrong
and needs our attention.

It teaches us what suffering feels like,
and so we learn to recognize pain
when we meet it in each other.

A friend of mine once said he could 'smell' unhappiness.
You only learn to smell unhappiness in others
when you have known the smell of unhappiness in yourself.
Only then can you feel with the other.

Pain begets compassion
and compassion shapes us into people
who are learning to be fully human.

And so we pray for each other.
When we feel helpless,
we bring each other to God,
begging that greater power than ours
might bring change and healing and wholeness
into the broken lives of those we love.

Because I need to remember

The human heart feels intensely,
suffers grievously,
rejoices exuberantly
and forgets easily.

One reason for praying is to help ourselves remember
the things that must not be forgotten,
but must be passed on
from generation to generation.

The earliest religious rituals of humankind
re-enacted sacred memories.

Intuitions of our cosmic beginnings,
remembered whenever we welcome a new child into
   the human family.

Celebrations of the power of love
to bind us together
in new networks of life,
re-enacted whenever we join in a wedding dance.

Leave-takings, and the relentless winds that blow us on
and bid us say 'Goodbye' at the cold graveside,
Or gather round the memory-stones
To repeat our heartfelt promises:
'We shall not let this happen ever again.'

We pray, lest we forget.

Because I want to speak my truth

Truth is something we all value,
yet find so elusive.

We know that the wholeness and harmony
of human living depend on truth and honesty,
yet we know we deceive each other
and we deceive ourselves.

It can begin with telling a lie,
And it can lead to living a lie.
It's not what we want,
but we can't disentangle ourselves
from the mazes of our own deceptions and self-deceptions.

In prayer we can speak our truth
and know that it will be received without judgment
   or rejection.

We can be furiously angry,
or we can release the passion of unrequited loving.

We can weep, in shame or in sorrow,
and we can erupt with happiness, like children at play.

We can name our fears and our desires,
and know that both are part of who we are,
and who we are is embraced in love by God.

In a world where we hardly dare appear,
even in our own homes,
without our protective masks,

what a relief to be ourselves,
nothing hidden,
nothing held back,

truly simple,
simply true.

To speak our honest truth
in the presence of God
can be the beginning of learning
to speak true to each other,
and to live true to ourselves.

Because I can't express what I feel

What do you say
when there are no words to say what you feel,
or what you mean
or what you want?

When the anxious mind finally wears itself out,
going round in circles.
When the anger is spent,
and there is no resolution.
When love dares not express itself
and the flow of the heart is forced underground.

Prayer speaks its truth in silence.
And the silence is understood
and enfolded back into the silences of space,
where its energy is not lost,
but transformed.

We pray when the words fail
and only silence suffices.

Who am I praying to?

Who am I praying to?

What kind of a question is that?

Either the answer is obvious...
or the question is unanswerable...
or both?

It has a very simple answer.
The simple answer is 'God'!

But it also has a multitude of very complex, and partial,
   and unsatisfactory answers.
Because no two people will ever really agree about
   'who' God is,
and each one of us will be growing and moving daily
   in our understanding
of who God is for us.

Yet our image of God will have a profound effect on
   the way we pray.
Just as our image of another person
affects the way we relate to that person,
what we say and how we say it,
and what we are likely to expect by way of a response.

Any idea or picture we have in our minds about 'God'
is inevitably going to be inadequate
and it may even be seriously misleading.

But prayer is meaningless
if it is just a form of words
spoken into thin air.
So we have something of a dilemma here.

We need to know that we are praying to Someone,
   who is real for us,
and yet we know that we can never really *know* the
   Mystery we call God.

God is always going to be bigger than any image
    we can form.
If it were not so, God would not be God.
The mystery is always going to lie beyond our rational
    comprehension,
as surely as the mind and heart of the playwright
will always be beyond the imagination of the actors
    on the stage,
and the vision of the composer will always be
    infinitely more
than the effect of a single bow upon a set of strings,
or a pair of hands upon a single keyboard.

If you doubt this, open up a volume of the complete works
    of Shakespeare;
run your finger along any line on any page.
Let your finger come to rest on any single letter
within any word of any sentence on that page.

Now imagine that all you could possibly know of the mind
    of Shakespeare
were in that single letter of a single word of all he wrote.
This gives us some idea of how little we can know of God,
relative to the Mystery of who God is.

And yet, knowing so little of the mind of a great playwright,
we are nevertheless stirred in our depths
by the power of his works.
We leave the theatre knowing that our hearts
    have been moved
and our lives changed, however imperceptibly,
by our encounter with this person's mind,
as it is expressed in his works.

Perhaps something like this is true
of our encounters with God.
We can know almost nothing
of the Mystery of God's mind and heart,
and yet our own hearts, and our own lives,
are profoundly affected
whenever we open ourselves up to the touch of this Mystery.

To pray is to connect to this Mystery,
yet to allow the Mystery to remain mystery.

This may mean that we have to shed,
or at least sit lightly to,
the many different, and partial, images of God
we have accumulated since our earliest attempts at prayer.

When we turn to God, in any particular situation,
it is worth asking ourselves what kind of god we are
   looking for
in that situation.

Are we looking for a satisfier of our shopping list requests?
Are we looking for a fireman to rescue us from
   an emergency?
Are we looking for a father figure to tell us what
   to do next?

And who is God for us in a more general way?

Is God an operations manager
who puts our plans into effect in the way we desire?

Is God a policeman or a strict head teacher,
always on the watch for us
to make a mistake
and lay ourselves open to punishment?
Clocking up our good and evil deeds
to decide whether we get through the entrance exam
    for heaven?

Or perhaps God is an employer,
who drains the last ounce of energy from us
and demands our unpaid overtime
in our efforts to 'do God's will'?

Or is God the fixer,
who keeps us safe,
solves our problems,
rearranges creation to suit our needs?

These are caricatures, of course,
and yet how easily, and how subtly, we slip into
one or other of these false and damaging images of God.

Because we are human, this will always be so,
    to some extent.
But to recognize the limitations of our images of God
is an important step to going beyond them.

It helps us to enter into the encounter with God
in the spirit of a loving relationship,
rather than a task that we have to accomplish.

It is the beginning of a lifelong relationship
which is being expressed in every moment,
in all we do and all we are and all we long for.

Just as the fish lives and moves and has its being in the water,
without needing to know what water is or where it
   came from,

just as the bird flies through the air without needing to know
how it is held, and propelled, by this invisible reality,

so we can live and move and have our being in God,
trusting the tides and currents of God's love,
that hold us, and move us, console and disturb us,
nourish, guide and challenge us.

To live in this reality
is to be in prayer
every moment.

Who are we praying to?
Certainly not some remote being in the sky,
who may or may not grant our requests.
Nor some authority figure
who may be with us or against us,
depending on how we behave.

When we pray,
we simply acknowledge
our longing to be in right relationship
with the source of all being.

All else follows from that fundamental choice.

When can I pray?

For most of us, it isn't a matter
of finding the *right* time for prayer,
but of finding any time at all.

The pressures are on us from all sides
to be *doing* so much
that there is no space or time left for simply *being*.

Yet a pattern of regular prayer
can be very helpful indeed,
and many people cherish a quiet time each day,
to recharge their batteries
and seek out the deeper presence of God in their lives.

If you can organize your day
to include some time for prayer,
you will be richly rewarded for your faithfulness.
The more generous we are in giving ourselves to God,
the more abundantly we will discover
God's action and power
in our living.

Maybe the early morning
is a good time for you to be still,
before the day's tasks take over.

Or at midday, as an oasis in the busyness.

Or at nightfall, to reflect on where God has been
in your life today.

Whatever time is good for you,
is a good time.

Time for prayer is time that is safe from interruption.
You may need to safeguard this time,
for example, by asking your family to respect it,
or by taking the phone off the hook.

Try, if you have a choice,
to find a time when you feel alert and attentive yourself.
This is going to be 'quality time'
and it asks for a 'quality you'.

Ten minutes of prayerful and alert awareness
will be far more fruitful
than an hour spent struggling to keep awake.

But what if this pattern of regular prayer simply isn't possible
in your life's schedule?

Authentic prayer can also be interwoven
into the events of every day.

This can be the beginning of
a life of prayer,
which may well lead to periods of focused meditation,
or, just as authentically,
may help you to realize
that everything you do and say
can be an act of prayer.

Let's begin with a habit of morning prayer
that takes almost no time at all,
but can help to reconnect us to God and to our world
after the darkness of sleep.

When you draw back the curtains on rising,
simply notice the sunrise,
or the simple fact that light has returned.

Receive this light with an open heart,
as a gift from the creator of all light
and as a gift from all the human family
living to the east of you.

You might like to remember, in your prayer,
anyone you know in these eastern regions,
or any countries in distress.

The light of life passes, like a baton in a relay race,
from east to west,
from time zone to time zone.

As you receive this gift, others are handing it on to you,
and seeking their own rest.
How will you use this gift during the next twelve hours?

Remember, for a moment, what you are intending to
    do today,
and ask God's blessing upon all that the day will bring,
whether planned or unplanned.

The energy of the sun,
whether we can actually see and feel it or not,
gives life to our bodies and our earth.

The energy of God,
whether we are aware of it or not,
makes our souls live
and invites all creation into the fullness of life.

The first moments of the day
can be a call to celebration and heartfelt gratitude,
concentrated into the moments it takes you to open
    your curtains,
but setting the tone for your whole day.

You can make this kind of prayer in reverse,
at nightfall,
when you draw the curtains closed again,
before retiring into the darkness
of a winter evening,
or a summer night.

Take a last look at the sunset,
or the waning light and lengthening shadows.
In your heart, pass the gift of light and life onwards
to all the human family
living to the west of you.

Remember anyone, or any region to the west
that lies especially on your heart.
As you prepare to rest,
they are just awakening to a new day.

What kind of world are you passing on to them?
Is it a little bit better than the one you received
   this morning
from your brothers and sisters in the east?
Or is it even more troubled than it was when you
   received it?

Parts of this world and its joys and sorrows
have been in your care this day.
How do you feel about how the day has gone?

Has the way you have lived this day
added to, or diminished,
the store of trust, of hope, of love in the world?

Don't make any judgments of yourself.
Simply acknowledge what you notice,
letting yourself become aware of any feelings of
   thankfulness,
or anxiety, or regret,
and allowing them to flow into the all-enfolding mystery
   of God.

Morning and evening are good times
to become consciously aware of your desire for God.
But what about the rest of the day?

You may feel that you are caught up
in a relentless flurry of activity and stress,
but there will always be pockets of stillness
if you know where to look for them.

Some of them will happen in spite of life's deadlines.

If you drive, you will certainly get stuck in traffic at times.

If you commute to work, you may spend quite some time
  each day
on trains or buses.

If you are a parent, you may spend time at the school gates
  every day,
waiting to take your child home.

Are there any times like these in your day?

How will you use that 'dead' time?
To curse the darkness, or to light a candle?

You can 'light a candle' by turning times of enforced
  idleness
into times of conscious prayer.

Other pockets of stillness can be freely chosen.

Even the busiest office routine allows for a coffee break.

Exercising the dog is an opportunity for 'walking prayer',
and exercising yourself can also be sacred time,
as you pedal the bike or pound the treadmill or jog around
    the park.

An hour at the swimming pool
can be an hour with God, who is holding you
even more surely than the water is supporting your body.

Amid the most pressing chores, you are still free
to take a five-minute walk in the garden or the park,
or to sit down, deliberately, and gratefully, for a few
    minutes' break on your own.

Even if you are 'never alone', you will bathe or shower
    from time to time,
and that too can become time for prayer,
as you let the cleansing water flow over and around you.

If your children never give you peace,
try spending five minutes in prayer
when you check on them before you go to bed.

As you listen to their breathing,
thanking God for the gift of their young lives,
you might commit your own life into God's hands too.

Whether your pocket of stillness is enforced or chosen,
you can turn it into prayer.

Begin by relaxing, and recognizing that there is nothing
   you can change in this situation.
Then allow your deeper thoughts and feelings to arise.

Is something troubling you? Name it and express it to
   yourself in the stillness.

Is someone on your mind? Let them pass into your prayer.

Or simply take a moment to look back on the day so far,
and notice anything that you are especially grateful about.

If you seriously desire to weave prayer into the fabric of
   your life,
all these times are opportunities to do just that.

To make a start,
just take note of any oasis times that arise in your daily
   routine today,
whether enforced or chosen,
and reflect on how you might turn them into times
   for prayer.

Where shall I pray?

Just as we may have grown up thinking
there is a 'right' time for prayer,
so we may have the idea that there is a 'right' place.

Maybe we think the 'right place'
is in a place of worship,
or in some especially 'holy' spot.

But the God who creates life
makes *every* place a sacred space,
because there is nowhere where God is not.

So we might approach the question of where to pray
from two directions.

It can be very helpful to have a favourite meeting place
    with God,
where we can go regularly
and feel especially open to the movements of the divine.

But it can be just as valid
to meet God in prayer
wherever we happen to find ourselves.

Many people like to have a place
that is a special prayer corner for them.

If this idea appeals to you,
your prayer place might be a little niche in your home.

If there is a corner where you can be sure you won't
   be disturbed,
and where you can spend time whenever you feel the
   desire or need for prayer,
you can make it into your own kind of sanctuary.

There are countless ways of doing this:
perhaps you might like to have a candle there,
which you light as a sign to yourself
that you are entering into prayer.

Or perhaps a fresh flower,
or some kind of image that connects you to God
or reminds you of times when you have felt that God
    has been close.

Of course, you can change these objects whenever
    you wish.
One day it might be the first of the daffodils to
    bloom in your garden,
another day you may feel you need to clutch a cross,
or focus on a photo of someone you want to pray for.

Let your heart guide you.
These objects are only there to help you connect to the
    deeper reaches of your heart.
Use what is helpful
and leave aside what is not.

If you are to be able to relax into the stillness of prayer,
you will need a firm, but comfortable, chair,
or a prayer stool, if you prefer,
or maybe a special cushion.

Be sure to give yourself a place to pray where you really
    can be relaxed,
as well as alert.
If you are uncomfortable,
you will find your mind is focusing on the discomfort
and this will distract you.

But if you are too comfortable,
you may well fall asleep,
and that can be a distraction too!
(Though, if you really do fall asleep during prayer,
don't worry!
you probably need the sleep,
and this may indeed be God's gift to you right now.
And in any case, God can touch us in our sleep
as surely as in our waking.)

Of course, this assumes that you are free to take over
   a corner of the home
and make it your own space.
This is by no means true for everyone.

If it is an impossibility for you,
then think about other spaces
where you feel you could spend quality time in prayer.

These may be outside the home.
Perhaps in the park, when the weather permits,
on a favourite bench,
or on a familiar walk.

A prayer place is really only a way
of focusing our hearts into prayer.
Is there another focus you could use?

Perhaps there is a tree in your garden,
that you can see from your window.
The tree will be growing and changing every day,
and expressing the movement of the seasons.
It can become your prayer companion.

Perhaps you spend a lot of time in your car.
Is there some way you can mark that place
as a place where you meet with God?

You might place some meaningful symbol on the dashboard,
where it will remind you of your special relationship
    with God
every time you catch sight of it.

In the same way, you might place a symbol
of your trust in God,
on your desk,
or beside the computer,
or on the kitchen window sill.

Perhaps the 'place' is somewhere that exists
only in your imagination.
Wherever you are,
you can close your eyes
and imagine yourself in a quiet space, alone with God,
however you envisage it.

The bus or train that takes you to work
or the jet aircraft that takes you overseas,
or the waiting room at the doctor's,
or the airport, or the hospital
can all be places of encounter with the living God.

This happens whenever you withdraw into the deepest
    reaches of your heart,
seeking stillness and the presence and guidance of God,
but it happens just as surely
whenever you notice God in action
in everything that is happening around you.

The cry 'Where is God?'
calls forth the echoing response, 'Everywhere is God'.

The more we can tune in to this echo,
the more we will discover God's presence in the world
   around us:

Not just in the beautiful,
but in the mundane.

In the jostle of the crowds,
and the exuberance of our children.

In the loneliness of the marginalized,
and the silent aching of those who grieve.

In the passionate embrace
and in the passionate debate.

In the storm clouds
as well as in the sunsets.

Every place
is sacred space,
because everywhere
is where God IS.

How do I pray?

There are as many ways of praying
as there are people desiring to pray.

There is no 'right' way,
and there are no 'wrong' ways.

A way of prayer is right,
if it is right for you
in the time and place and circumstances
where you find yourself.

A way of prayer is right
if it draws you closer into living relationship with God,
the kind of relationship that makes a difference,
to what you say and do,
and who you are.

So try out any of these suggestions
and see how they feel for you.

Use this section
as you would use a menu card in a restaurant.
Taste whatever appeals to you,
and enjoy!

And remember that there are countless 'dishes'
that are not on this menu card at all.
So remain open to whatever God will continue to
    open up for you
in all the surprises of living and loving.

Becoming still

Whatever kind of prayer you are making,
and however you are feeling,
you will need to take at least a moment
to become inwardly still.
This isn't always as easy as it sounds,
but it is well worth the effort,
whether you are consciously trying to pray, or not.
Three good ways to do this are:

Relax

Breathe

Listen

Relax

If your life is one long round of busyness,
try simply noticing, every so often,
the tension in your muscles,
especially your neck and shoulders.

Wherever you are,
just relax those muscles for a moment.
Sit back in your office chair,
or stand at ease in the supermarket checkout,
and let those muscles relax.
You will notice the difference immediately.

As you relax,
remind yourself that your being is held
in Something, or Someone,
much greater than yourself.
For a moment, let your thoughts revolve around
   this simple truth:

'I have my being in an ocean of love.
Just as my physical being began in an embryonic sac,
which provided me with all I needed,
and was enfolded in a womb that protected and held me
and prepared me for a fuller life beyond the womb,
so, even now, my inner self is held in an ocean of love,
which I cannot see or understand, but I can trust.'

Breathe

We don't need to be reminded to breathe,
but we can learn to be more conscious
of this precious gift of the breath of life.

Wherever you are,
and whatever you are doing,
take a minute to become aware of your own breathing.
Don't change its rhythm, just notice it.
Just doing this will help you to become more calm,
and refresh your perspective on life.
It will also come as a relief to your body,
and may even reduce your blood pressure.

Now take it a step further:

Each time you breathe out,
consciously let go, or express, any anxiety or concerns
  you may have.

Each time you breathe in,
breathe in the power and the love of God,
and the life of God's creation,
which sustains you constantly,
whether you are aware of it or not.

Practise this rhythm for a few minutes,
whenever you have an opportunity.
Return to it whenever you can,
and especially whenever you are feeling stressed.

Listen

The world is alive with the music of life.

The act of listening,
deeply and attentively,
to the sounds around you,
and within you,
is a very good way of coming to inner stillness.

Begin by noticing the sounds in the distance,
the traffic,
the roar of a jet plane,
the rumble of thunder,
the bustle of the crowds.

Then move the focus closer to home:
the creaking of the floorboards,
the hum of the computer,
the chatter of children.
Notice every sound, and every murmur.

Finally,
move the focus inside yourself.
Tune in to the beating of your heart,
the steady rhythm of your pulse.

Just as your heart's action
keeps your body alive,
so your eternal self is held in being,
moment by moment,
by the heart of God.

When I'm concerned about someone

'Say one for me.'
It's a request we may make lightly,
or it may really be spoken from the heart.
Sometimes, another person,
maybe a loved one,
or even someone who is giving us grief,
lies upon our heart
and we know that prayer is needed.

Imagine yourself in that person's home.
In your prayer, sit down beside them.
Allow their situation to fill your heart,
knowing that God is receiving it.
As you go deeper, with God,
you are carrying the other person with you,
trusting that in the heart of God there is healing
    and wholeness.

Stop to think:

Can you do anything practical for the person you are
    praying for?
Can you become an answer to your own prayer?

When I'm concerned about our world

As you read the newspaper
or hear the daily news on radio or television,
does any particular item leap out at you?

Perhaps the situation seems simply too big to handle,
too remote, too desperate?
Yet your heart registers its concern.

Try focusing on one real human aspect of the matter,
one person's face you have seen on your TV screen,
one personal detail, one family in trouble,
one city dealing with devastation.

Take those images,
and your own feelings about them,
into the consciousness of God's presence,
which is at the heart of prayer.

As you draw closer to God,
you carry those people and situations to God with you.
You are making an invisible lifeline across the world
and you may never know the effects.

Stop to think:

Is there any practical help you can give
to bring a little humanity into the situation you are
   praying for?

When I'm desperate

Perhaps family relationships are at breaking point,
or the loneliness is just too hard to bear,
or the pain won't let go its grip on you.

Perhaps fear is crippling you,
or you are standing, bewildered, in the face of a dilemma.

Express your feelings, just as they are.
sit down with God,
or retreat into a quiet corner
and let the desperation rise to the surface of your mind.

Simply facing it, and naming it,
in the presence of God,
may be the first step to moving beyond it.

Stillness alone won't fix anything,
but it may lead to a shift in perspective.

When the train of your life is on a collision course,
prayer may help you to change the points
and find a new direction.

Stop to think:

In this desperate situation, what do I actually,
   deep down, *desire?*
For myself, *and for others?*
What might be my next step towards helping this desire
   to be fulfilled?

When I don't know what to say to God

You feel the need for prayer,
yet, when it comes to the point,
you can't put your needs, your feelings, your concerns
into words.

The good news is
our hearts don't need words.
They have a language of their own,
which is the language of God.

If you don't know what to say,
say nothing at all.

Simply be still, with the silence.
The time comes, for all of us,
when words fade into silence,
and the silence can open us to the presence of God,
more powerfully than any number of words.

Let the eternal Word receive your silent yearnings.
Listen to the sound of silence.

Stop to think:

How comfortable are you with silence?
Do you feel the need for a constant background of sound
    in the house?
If you are afraid of silence, take it gently, just a few minutes
    at a time,
until you feel more at home with it.

When I've got heaps to say to God

On the other hand,
sometimes you'll have so much to say
that your outpourings will flow like a river.

God is the perfect listener.
Don't hesitate to let it all come out.

But it can be good, too, to let God have a go.
Try letting your prayer become a conversation,
just as it might be with an old and trusted friend –
the kind of friend you can say anything to,
and know they won't stop loving you –
the kind of friend who can challenge you,
without endangering your friendship.

God can certainly deal with your monologues,
but a dialogue might be more fruitful.

Stop to think:

A significant conversation with a good friend never leaves
    us unchanged.
In what ways do you feel your conversation with God
    is changing you,
challenging you, affirming or consoling you?

When I'm furious with God

Sacred scripture is full of stories
of people throwing the book at God
and really letting God bear the brunt of their anger.
God is quite big enough to cope with this!
God has broad shoulders,
broad enough for all of us to cry on,
and broad enough to be a universal punchbag.

Don't suppress your anger
until it goes inwards, and makes you depressed,
or turns outwards into words or acts of violence.

In your prayer you can tell it how it really is.
Rage and wrestle with God as much as you need to
and don't even think about feeling guilty about it!

But in all your raging,
try to make a little oasis of stillness before you go back
to 'normal life'.

Let the force of your anger break over God
like a wave on the beach,
but then let there be a moment of stillness
  as the wave recedes.

Stop to think:

What is the root cause of your anger?
Is there any way you can address this root cause?
If you need practical human help, are you ready
  to go and ask for it?

When I'm 'off' God altogether...

Even the great saints and mystics of old
had their 'off' times.
Sometimes God seems to be a million miles away
and we don't even know whether we want
anything to do with God, ever again.
Maybe we feel life has dealt us a rough deal,
and we blame God for it,
consciously or unconsciously.

Maybe the old ways of praying, or of practising formal religion,
just don't work for us any more,
or we feel betrayed by religious institutions
and we have no desire whatever for prayer.

Two approaches can be helpful in this situation:

The first is to stay with the habit of prayer, regardless,
just as you stay in an old friendship, and keep on nourishing it,
even if it seems to have lost its sparkle.

The second is to recognize that we are growing and moving
and that nothing is fixed in concrete,
especially not our relationship with God.
Maybe the time has come to try new ways of letting ourselves
be aware of God as the Mystery that enfolds us.

... and feeling disconnected

Try standing under the stars,
and letting your heart reach out,
like an invisible thread,
to connect to each one of them.
You are part of this vast and beautiful universe.

Take time out in your garden or the park,
walk into the hills or woods, or beside the sea,
become aware of the pulse of life that pushes
    the sap up in springtime
and makes the bulbs grow
and keeps the tides flowing and ebbing.
You are part of it all.

Try making a deliberate link with someone,
an old friend maybe, or even an old enemy,
the person next door,
the colleague across the office,
the homeless person on the street,
another parent waiting at the school gates,
another patient in the waiting room.
We are all held in a web of interrelatedness.
You are part of it.
Your part matters.

Stop to think:

However you feel,
nothing can separate you from the wholeness of creation,
and God is the name we give to that Mystery.

When I'm sitting at my desk

Whatever your work is,
you can do it with a wider, and deeper, awareness.

What are you really doing
and why are you doing it?
Let your reasons for doing it flow into prayer.
Perhaps you are working to support a family?
Let them be a focus for prayer.
Perhaps you are engaged in a project, or a vocation,
that makes a difference to other people's lives?
Bring this awareness into your prayer.
Perhaps you are bored out of your mind?
An empty mind is a place that can, potentially,
become filled with the stillness and presence of God.
Try letting this happen.

If you use a computer, try praying with the internet.
A good place to start is with a web site called
    'Sacred Space', on http:www.jesuit.ie/prayer.
A few minutes spent on a site like this
could make a big difference to your day.

Stop to think:

Two medieval stone masons were asked,
    'What are you doing?'
One replied, 'I'm laying one stone upon another.'
The other replied, 'I'm building a cathedral.'

What do *you* think you are doing?

When I'm too tired

Prayer is about receiving a gift,
more than about making a huge effort.

So it's the end of a long day,
and you're exhausted.
All you want to do is chill out, or sleep.

Or maybe life itself is like a long, exhausting day.
You have no energy for prayer.

Try noticing how God is carrying you.
Turn this into practice by letting yourself sink,
deeply and consciously,
with all your weight,
lower and lower
into your chair, or your bed,
and noticing how it feels to be really held.

A baby 'prays' like this as she lies in her mother's arms.
A toddler 'prays' like this as his father carries him home
on broad, strong shoulders.

It is the prayer of absolute trust
and God will never fail to respond to it.

Stop thinking about it. Just be!

So far, in this section,
we have looked at some ways of praying
as it were 'in flight',
in different moods and situations.

But, of course, there is huge treasure
to be discovered in more sustained forms of prayer.

You might like to try some of the 'recipes' that follow.
Use anything that is helpful.
Leave aside anything that isn't.

How was your day?

This is a form of prayer, sometimes called the *Examen*,
that has been practised by Christians for many centuries.

Take a few minutes of quiet time
to look back
over the past twenty-four hours.

Does anything arise in your memory?
Maybe something specially good happened
or something unpleasant that disturbed you.

Just notice these things.
Don't make any judgments.

Our reactions to what happens
can help us see
what is leading us closer
to our true centre in God,
and what is pulling us
further away from that true centre.

What do your feelings show you?
What happened today
to draw you closer to God?
Did anything leave you
feeling less centred, more fragmented?

Notice what makes you feel
more alive, more at one
with other people, and all creation,
more 'whole',
and nourish these parts of your life.

Notice what tends to deaden you,
alienate you from others,
or make you self-absorbed.

Just noticing these things
will help you to work against them.

What we nourish,
by giving it our attention and our energy,
will grow.

What we leave aside,
depriving it of our attention and our energy,
will shrink.

Which parts of your life do you want to grow?
How are you nourishing that growth?

Try to find one thing that has given you joy.
Thank God especially for that thing.

Try to find one aspect of the day that you can feel proud of.
Honour that moment – your gifts are from God.
To honour them and to use them
is to honour God and serve God's creation.

End your prayer
by entrusting tomorrow
to the One who gave you today.

Praying with scripture

Scripture is much more than a set of books,
to be read, and believed,
or used in evidence of a particular belief system.

Scripture captures the essence
of what humankind has struggled to express of God.

Whatever your own faith background,
scripture can be a powerful resource for prayer.

We can soak ourselves in just a single phrase of it,
savouring it until we have imbibed its meanings.
Or we can enter into its stories,
as if we were actually there,
letting them affect us
as they affected those
who were physically present at the time.

Lectio divina

We can soak ourselves in scripture
using the ancient art of *lectio divina*.

This means, very simply…

Reading, and rereading, a passage of scripture,
or listening carefully,
as it is read, and reread,
until we find a phrase that seems to jump out at us from
   the page,
attracting our closer attention.

Meditating on the chosen phrase
until it reveals its personal significance for us.
What attracted us to this particular text at all
and how does it connect to where we actually find ourselves
in the circumstances of our daily living?

Applying the wisdom of the text,
as discovered in our prayer,
to the encounters and relationships of our lives
and the choices we are making, moment by moment.

Imaginative meditation

We can enter into a scriptural story or event,
as if we were physically present to it,
by using our imagination.

This is the prayer of imaginative meditation.

Choose any story or event from scripture.
Read it through, and become really familiar with it.

Now let yourself become inwardly still
and imagine you are there at the scene.

Don't try to reconstruct the landscape of long ago,
but let the scene take place wherever your
   imagination suggests.

Let yourself explore the sounds and sights,
the smells and the atmosphere of the scene.
It may help to imagine that you are describing it
   to someone else.

Notice who is there in your scene.
If your scripture is from the gospels, where is Jesus
   in the scene?
Where are *you* in the scene?

Don't try to stage-manage your scene.
Even if you don't entirely like what you see,
let it be as it is.
It may have something important to reveal to you,
just as it is.

What you are imagining is coming up
from deeper layers of your psyche,
and may help you to notice what is really important to you
and how you are really feeling.

As you 'inhabit' the scene,
how do you want to react to it?

Is there anyone there you would like to talk with?
If so, let your prayer become a conversation.
Express, freely, anything you are feeling.

The stories of sacred scripture
have a special power to connect right into our own
    lived experience.

By entering into them imaginatively and prayerfully,
we can discover these connections for ourselves.

For example,
we may discover that we tend to keep out of the limelight,
or avoid getting involved.
or that we tend to rush in regardless,
to act first and think later.

In what specific ways does your experience
in this scene, or event, or encounter,
connect with what is going on in your own life?
What can you learn from it
about yourself? About your place in the world?
About the direction of your life, or simply the next step
    to take?

Creative prayer

Prayer doesn't have to be about words,
or even just about silence.

Prayer can flow from, and through,
everything we do.
God's creative impulse,
to express something of Godself in creation,
also finds expression in our own creativity.

What particular creative gifts have been entrusted to *you*?

Perhaps you enjoy making, or listening to, music?
If so, listen to God's inweaving of Godself,
as you listen to the kind of music you enjoy the most.
Is it speaking to your heart?
How would you wish to respond?
Let your response become prayer,
which may itself be expressed in song,
or dance,
or a poem,
or a piece of music of your own.

Perhaps you enjoy painting and visual art?
If so, try praying with your pencils or paints,
or a lump of clay.
Allow what is deep within you
to find expression through these media.

You don't have to be 'artistic' to do this.
It isn't about producing a masterpiece,
but about allowing the deeper movements within you
to find outward expression.

If you can share the results with a trusted friend,
so much the better.

Prayer can flow profoundly
as you wander round a gallery,
or browse through an illustrated book.
Linger with any image that seems to speak to you.

Why is it important to you?
How might this experience help you to grow inwardly,
or relate more meaningfully to those around you?

Or try meeting God at the theatre or cinema,
or a video night at home, or a good novel or favourite poem.

Images, drama and music touch layers of our being
that lie deeper than rational thought.
They expose us to the heart of God in special ways.

To meet God in these ways
is to be in prayer,
just as surely as when we are
focused on sacred scripture
or in the silence of contemplation.

To gaze at your sleeping child,
Or to gaze at the sweeping stars,
Is to gaze into an icon of God.

To stop to smell the roses
or to savour the scent of wood smoke
is to inhale the incense of God's breath,
bringing life to the world.

To listen with love,
as another pours out his heart,
to touch another with tenderness and compassion,
as she fights back her tears,
is to attend to the world with God's ears,
and touch the world with God's fingers.

Praying with others

We are, by our very nature, relational creatures,
who have evolved to connect with each other,
with the world… and with God.

So sometimes we may wish to pray together,
perhaps in a small group of two or three,
perhaps in a larger group of people
with a common basis of faith.

Together we share our needs and concerns,
not forgetting to notice the practical ways we can help
and support each other.

Together we reflect on what is wrong in our hearts,
in the way we function as a group, or in society,
the way we cherish, or fail to cherish, our planet home
and all the life upon it.

Together we allow the feelings inside us to overflow
in joyful response to all that lies around and beyond us,
sometimes quietly, sometimes exuberantly.

Together we share the depth of silence,
perhaps in circles of contemplative prayer.

Together we re-enact the defining moments
of our shared and sacred story.

And together we can turn our prayer into action.

Alone I can do very little.
Together there is very little that we cannot do.

The dreaded distractions

Distractions in prayer get more attention than they deserve!

They make us feel guilty.
They make us feel we have failed.
They undo our careful efforts to relax.
They shift our focus, in seconds,
from eternity
to the milk we left boiling on the gas ring.

Some distractions need immediate attention.
If you left something on the boil,
go and see to it! Then come back to prayer.

If you suddenly think of all the other things you should
   be doing,
just acknowledge the thoughts,
file them under 'see to it later',
and then come back to prayer.

If a distraction keeps on and on at you,
reminding you of a particular anxiety in your life,
maybe that distraction is actually an invitation
to bring that concern right into the heart of your prayer.

A wise friend once told me,
'Distractions are like birds flying round your head.
You can't stop them flying,
but you don't have to let them build a nest in your hair.'

Soul friendship

A very special kind of togetherness
is the gift of soul friendship.

A soul friend is one to whom we can open our hearts,
fully, and without reservation,
knowing that we are in safe and sacred space.

A soul friend listens with genuine attentiveness
to our story,
and helps us, in our telling of it,
to glimpse its holiness.

We can share our spiritual journey,
and know that we will not be judged or reproached,
though we may be challenged
and encouraged to take the step we dare not take alone.

Soul friendship is a gift we can both give and receive.
Do you have someone who is a soul friend to you?
If not, look around your circle of acquaintances.
Is there someone who might fulfil this role for you?

Are you a soul friend to anyone?
If not, be open to the possibility
that you might be invited into this sacred trust.

Making a retreat

A retreat is simply a sustained period of time
given over to deepening your journey with God.

It may be as short as a day in a quiet place,
or as long as several days, or even weeks,
'away from it all', in seclusion.

Or it may be a special kind of prayer journey
interwoven with your daily life and work,
in your own home, at your own pace,
with a sensitive companion, or soul friend,
whom you meet regularly
to share whatever is happening for you.

It may be silent,
or it may give you a chance to meet like-minded people.
The choice is yours.

A retreat can bring a breath of fresh air
into the stalemate of a stalled journey,
and it can release new energy
to keep you going, and growing.

Does it work?

To ask whether prayer 'works'
is to think of prayer as some kind of machine,
or solution to fix a problem.

Anyone who has ever prayed
for a particular outcome
will know how it feels when God doesn't 'answer' the prayer.

When this happens,
we may need to ask ourselves, again,
who God is for us.

If our dominant (though unconscious) image of God
is a kind of Santa Claus,
we may well be disappointed if God doesn't give us
    what we asked for.

If God is a 'parent', there to tell us what to do,
or to provide us with absolute security,
we may feel bewildered when no obvious guidance
    is forthcoming,
or when we feel very insecure and vulnerable.

But if, in prayer, we are truly seeking relationship
with the God who is Mystery,
yet dwells in our own hearts,
and moves and acts in everything we do and are,
then prayer will always deepen that relationship.

We may not see or feel any immediate change,
but authentic prayer always makes a difference.
It changes our attitudes,
and transforms our vision, of ourselves,
our relationships and our world.

Others may sense the change in us,
even when we cannot see it in ourselves.
We will know the power of prayer by its fruits,
though these fruits may be a long while in ripening.
Hard hearts may soften,
old resentments yield to new compassion,
breakdown lead to breakthrough.

Prayer that works
is prayer that makes a difference,
contemplation that turns into action,
on behalf of peace and justice
in a troubled and unjust world system.

Prayer is energy,
the energy of love and transformative power.

It is given to us to use for the good of all creation.
In prayer God gives us the fuel of life,
and asks us to live it.